THINGS TO MAKE FROM AUTUMN SEEDS AND LEAVES

"Season of mists and mellow fruitfulness"

Keats

THINGS TO MAKE FROM AUTUMN SEEDS AND LEAVES

Devised and drawn

by

ROSALIE BROWN

JADE PUBLISHERS
HASLEMERE

Jade Publishers
15 Stoatley Rise
Haslemere
Surrey GU27 1AF

First published 1989

Cover illustration by Nick Garner

Typeset by 'Keyword', Aldbury, Herts.
Printed and bound by MacLehose & Partners Ltd, Portsmouth.

British Library Cataloguing in Publication Data
Brown, Rosalie, 1910–
Things to make from autumn seeds and leaves.
1. Handicrafts using seeds. Handicrafts using leaves
I. Title
745.92'8

ISBN 0–903461–15–3

FOREWORD

This book is different from most of the others in my *Things to Make* series, because the crafts I describe in those books can be made all the year round, whereas, as the title suggests, the crafts in this book are made from seeds and leaves which can usually only be found during autumn and winter months.

Years ago, children did not have 'ready-made' toys to play with as they do today, so they made up their own activities and games from the different seeds and leaves which they found under the trees and firs in gardens, parks and fields. Over the years I have shown a great many children how to make these figures, birds, animals, and so on, and all have been fascinated and amused by the results.

So, when you go out for a walk, take a bag with you and drop into it any seeds, cones and leaves you find. To help you identify them, I have included four pages of illustrations of seeds and leaves with their tree names (pp.12–15). Then, when you get home, lay them out to dry off on a newspaper. If you can't lay them out immediately, keep them in a paper bag, *not* a plastic bag; seeds and leaves tend to go mouldy if kept in plastic bags.

This is important: to make leaves dry flat, *press them all separately* between sheets of newspaper, under a heavy weight. Books are excellent for this; they can be very heavy when stacked in a pile.

Other materials will be needed to help make these crafts. Quite a lot can be found at home, but some, such as pipecleaners, liquid glue, and so on, may have to be bought. Tube glue is not suitable for these crafts but it is possible to buy liquid glues and gums which do well. The materials you will need are listed on page 11.

Near the end of the book you will find pages of toys and games, with the rhymes children said when playing them. There is also the translation of a rhyme from Germany which was given to me.

You may not find in your area all the seeds, cones and leaves mentioned to make the various items illustrated, but the drawings and notes will help you to make up your own ideas from what you do find. Two things to remember: first, red berries do not keep their smooth, shiny skin very long; and second, *Never* use squashy soft fruits and berries like raspberries.

And finally, a safety warning:

Never eat any of the berries you find.

ROSALIE BROWN

CONTENTS

(Cont.)

MATERIALS USED
IN THESE HANDCRAFTS

10 pence coin
Bradawl (if needed)
Brown wrapping paper
Calendars
Cardboard
Cardboard plates
Cellophane with
  gummed back
Clear gum
Cloth for 'darts'
Coloured drinking straws
Coloured felt pens
Coloured papers
Coloured wool
Corrugated paper (card)
Cotton thread
Cotton wool
Feathers
Gummed paper
  (white or coloured)
Knitting needle
Large bead
Lollystick
Matchboxes
Matchsticks (used)
Needle with large eye
Newspaper

Pencil and rubber
Pinking shears
Pins, small
Pins, small with round
  coloured heads
Pipecleaners
Plate or saucer
  (for drawing circles)
Plastic container top
Plastic trays
  (from packed foods)
Plasticine
Postcards, plain
Poster paint
Ribbon or tape
Round cheeseboxes
Ruler
Scissors
Small beads or marbles
Small cardboard boxes
Small round lids
Square of felt material
String
Thimble
Thin wire or hairpin
White or coloured card
White sheet of paper

TREE LEAVES AND THEIR SEEDS

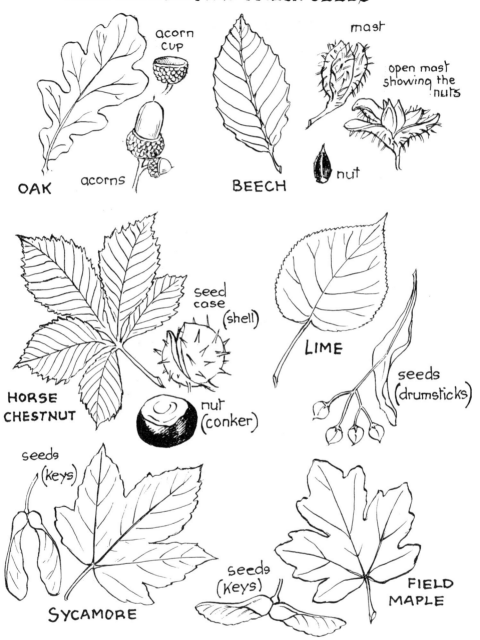

acorn cup

mast

open mast showing the nuts

nut

OAK   acorns

BEECH

seed case (shell)

LIME

HORSE CHESTNUT

nut (conker)

seeds (drumsticks)

seeds (keys)

SYCAMORE

seeds (keys)

FIELD MAPLE

TREE LEAVES AND THEIR SEEDS

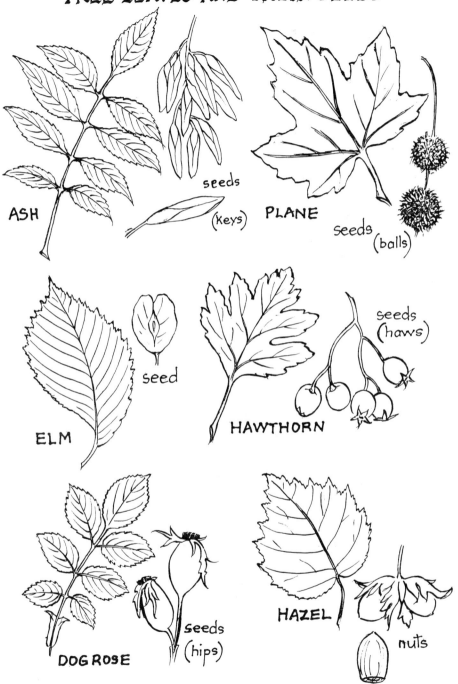

ASH

seeds (keys)

PLANE

seeds (balls)

ELM

seed

HAWTHORN

seeds (haws)

DOG ROSE

seeds (hips)

HAZEL

nuts

TREE LEAVES AND THEIR SEEDS

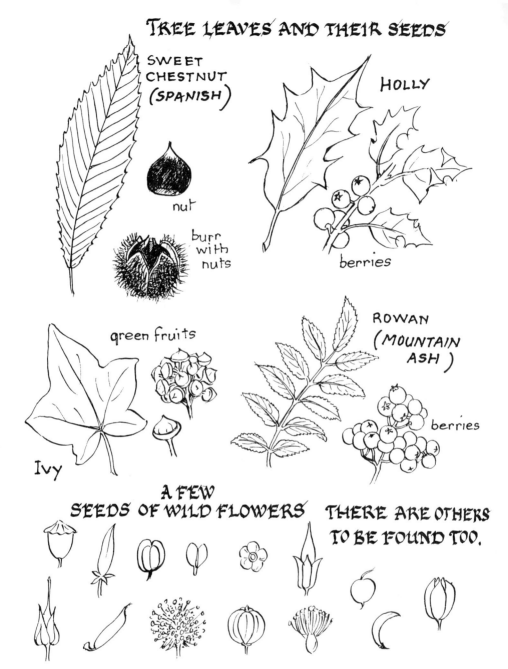

SWEET CHESTNUT (SPANISH)

nut

burr with nuts

HOLLY

berries

green fruits

Ivy

ROWAN (MOUNTAIN ASH)

berries

A FEW SEEDS OF WILD FLOWERS

THERE ARE OTHERS TO BE FOUND TOO.

FIRS AND THEIR CONES

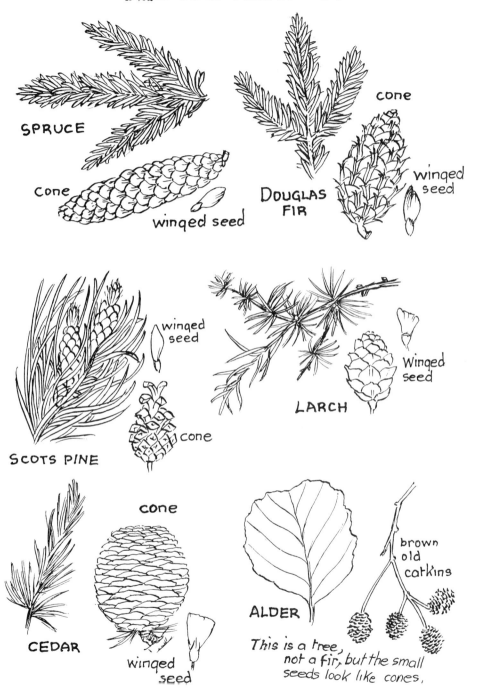

SPRUCE

cone

winged seed

DOUGLAS FIR

cone

winged seed

SCOTS PINE

winged seed

cone

LARCH

Winged seed

CEDAR

cone

winged seed

ALDER

brown old catkins

This is a tree, not a fir, but the small seeds look like cones,

FUNNY CREATURES

Materials: a. Beech nuts and mast   b. Matchsticks
                  c. Sweet chestnut burrs   d. Pipecleaners
                  e. Acorns and cups   f. Plasticine
                  g. Twigs   h. Melon seeds
                  i. Feathers   j. Rose hip
                  k. Knitting needle to   l. Cedar cone
                     make holes   (or other large cone)
                  m Glue or gum   n. Small round seeds
                  o. Small cones   p. Cardboard, papre
                     such as larch

A.   Stick the beechmast on to an acorn head. Sharpen the ends of matchsticks and push them into holes made in the sweet chestnut body for necks, arms and legs.

B.   Glue the beechmast collar to the cedar cone. Make a hole in the bottom of the acorn (the head) and push the short stump of the beech mast into it. Glue.

C.   *Shepherd.* Use a long pipecleaner for his shepherd's crook; it will also help the shepherd to stand. Make holes in his body to push in and glue pipecleaners for arms and legs. Make a matchstick neck as for **A.**

D.   *Parrot.* For the parrot's perch make a small cut in the top of a long twig (D1) and glue the short twig into it (D2). Push the end of the long twig into plasticine and then into the centre of the square card. Glue the parrot's head (a rosehip or acorn) firmly to the cone body and then glue the body onto the perch. Add a beechnut beak and feathers.

E.   *Stork.* This is made in the same way as the other creatures, but its long pipecleaner legs are bent into a round shape (E1). Stick paper over this shape, draw on three long strokes for claws and cut out a webbed foot shape.

FUNNY CREATURES

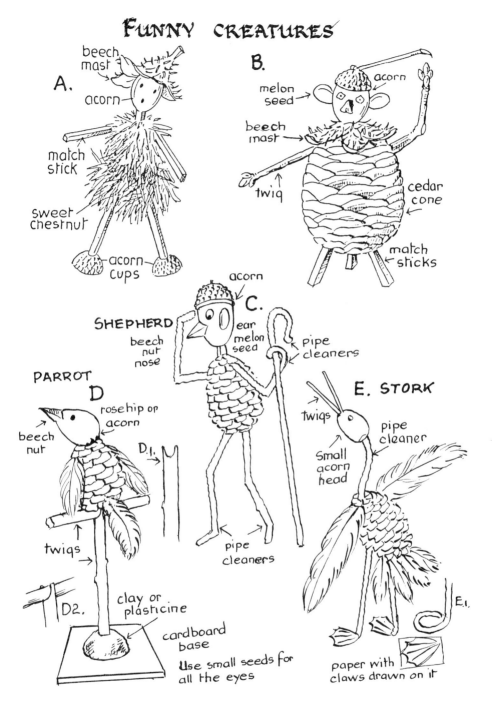

A.
- beech mast
- acorn
- match stick
- sweet chestnut
- acorn cups

B.
- melon seed
- acorn
- beech mast
- twig
- cedar cone
- match sticks

SHEPHERD **C.**
- acorn
- ear melon seed
- beech nut nose
- pipe cleaners

PARROT **D**
- beech nut
- rosehip or acorn
- D.1.
- twigs
- D2.
- clay or plasticine
- cardboard base
- Use small seeds for all the eyes
- pipe cleaners

E. STORK
- twigs
- pipe cleaner
- Small acorn head
- E.1.
- paper with claws drawn on it

FUNNY BIRDS

Materials:
a. 'Conkers'
b. String
c. Beech mast
d. Plasticine
e. Acorns and cups
f. Thin wire
g. Fir cones
h. Liquid glue or gum
i. Sycamore 'keys'
j. Feathers
k. Small seeds
l. Pipecleaners
m. Hazel nut
n. Grass
o. Small twigs or matchsticks
p. Knitting needle to make holes

All Birds

Make holes with a knitting needle and push pipecleaners and sharpened matchsticks into the bird bodies. It is easy to see from the pictures how to make birds **A**, **B** and **F**.

C. *Ostrich*. To make the neck, thread acorns onto wire or a hairpin and push this into the head and body. Use grass or feathers for the tail.

D. This bird has a colourful red rosehip head. Its legs are bent twigs if you can find some of the right shape; if not, use pipecleaners.

E. Thread a needle with thin string or strong cotton. Knot it first at one end and push it though the pine cone body. Tie the other end of the string or cotton to a stick. Swing this to make the bird 'fly'.

18

FUNNY BIRDS

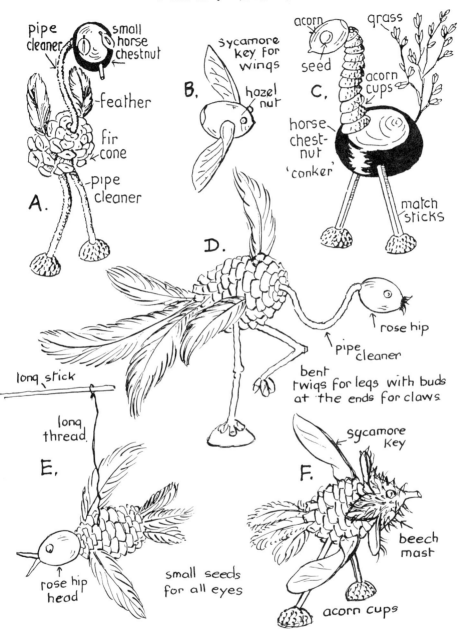

A.
pipe cleaner
small horse chestnut
feather
fir cone
pipe cleaner

B.
sycamore key for wings
hazel nut

C.
acorn
grass
seed
acorn cups
horse-chest-nut 'conker'
match sticks

D.
rose hip
pipe cleaner
bent twigs for legs with buds at the ends for claws

E.
long stick
long thread
rose hip head
small seeds for all eyes

F.
sycamore key
beech mast
acorn cups

MORE FUNNY CREATURES

Materials:
a. 'Conkers'	b. Small pins
c. Rose hips	d. Liquid glue or gum
e. Sycamore 'keys'	f. Knitting needle
g. Melon seeds	h. Matchsticks
i. Plane 'ball'	j. Pipecleaners
k. Hazel nuts	l. Elm seeds
m. Acorn cups	n. Wire or hair pin
o. Small round seeds or beads	p. Small twiggy 'branches'
q. Beechmast and seeds	

All Animals

Small round seeds or beads are used for all the eyes. Use the glue to stick eyes and ears in place. Use the knitting needle to make holes in the bodies to insert the legs and tails. For these, sharpen matchsticks at one end and push in, or use twigs.

A. Glue the beechmast 'head' to the body.

B. Glue the conkers together for the body.

C. Use small twiggy bits to make the antlers.

D. Glue plane balls firmly together to make the body.

E. The neck is made of acorn cups threaded on to the wire or a hair pin which is then pushed into the body and head.

MORE FUNNY CREATURES

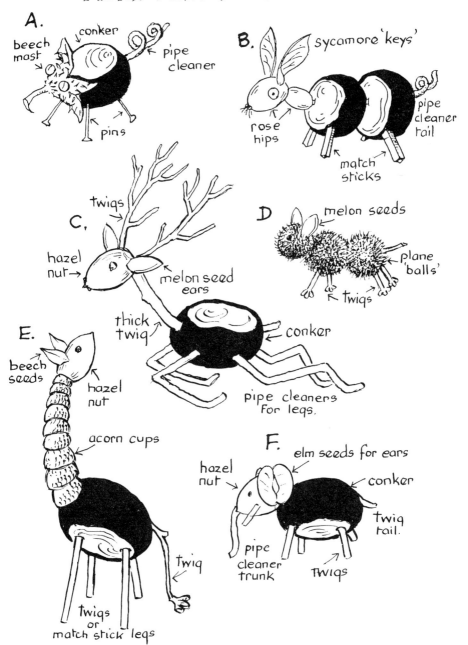

A. conker, beech mast, pipe cleaner, pins

B. sycamore 'keys', rose hips, pipe cleaner tail, match sticks

C. twigs, hazel nut, melon seed ears, thick twig, conker, pipe cleaners for legs.

D. melon seeds, plane 'balls', twigs

E. beech seeds, hazel nut, acorn cups, twig, twigs or match stick legs

F. elm seeds for ears, conker, hazel nut, twig tail, pipe cleaner trunk, twigs

POPPY SEEDHEAD FIGURES

Materials: a. Poppy seed heads on long stalks
                b. Gummed coloured paper
                c. Acorn cups   d. Scissors
                e. Plasticine   f. Pipecleaners
                g. Leaves (large and small)
                h. Ruler   i. Liquid glue or gum
                j. Knitting needle   k. Black felt pen

All Figures

Twist a pipecleaner under a seed head and glue firmly. Leave about 5cm (2") of stem for the bodies and glue another pipecleaner round them near the bottom to make legs. The diagram shows this clearly with dotted lines under skirt, shorts and dress. Draw faces on all figures with the black felt pen.

A.   *Dancer.* If you like, glue on small leaves for hands, and glue on two pretty leaves for her skirt. The ones used here are hawthorn leaves. Bend the arms and legs into position and push one foot into a ball of plasticine. Flatten this down firmly to make the dancer stand up.

B.   *Acrobat.* To make his shorts fold a piece of paper in half (B1). Draw on a 'shorts' shape and cut through both halves of paper together. Stick the shorts (B2) over the body and legs. Glue on small leaves for his hands. Push plasticine on the top of his head so he can stand on it upside down.

C.   *Another Acrobat.* This acrobat can have shorts too, cut the same way in paper as for B1 and B2. Push his lower hand into plasticine.

D.   *Girl.* Measure her body from arms to below the twisted part of the legs. Cut a length of coloured gummed paper twice that length but only wide enough to go across from arm to arm. Fold the paper in half and on one side draw this dress outline, with the fold at the top (D1). Cut both halves of paper together. Now cut along the fold to make it easier to stick both halves of the dress together over the body. Push plasticine into the bottom of the acorn cups and make holes at the top. Push her feet into these holes so she will stand up.

POPPY SEEDHEAD FIGURES

A.

small leaf for the hands

pipe cleaner arms and legs

two leaves for the skirt

small leaf for the hands

B.

B.1. folded paper

B.2.

leaf over end of pipe cleaner

plasticine here

C.

clay or plasticine

width of arms

D.1. folded paper

D.

acorn cup feet with plasticine pushed inside.

ACORN NOVELTIES

Materials:
    a. Many acorns, some with cups and some without
    b. Larch cone or other small cone
    c. Small seeds for ears and eyes
    d. Sycamore 'keys'   e. Cotton wool
    f. Round seeds   g. Needle and thread
    h. Drinking straw   i. Liquid glue or gum
    j. Matchsticks   k. Pipecleaners
    l. Knitting needle to   m. Black felt pens
      make holes

A. *Small Snake.* Arrange the cups in sizes, largest ones near the head. Thread a double length of cotton. Tie a large knot and push the needle into an acorn, then through each cup down to the small one (A1). Pull the thread tight so each cup fits into each other (A2) and fasten off with another knot. Glue on two small round seeds for eyes.

B. *Large Snake.* Arrange the acorns in sizes, largest to smallest. Again thread the needle with a double length of cotton as in A1. Push the needle through the cone and into each acorn. Pull tight and tie a knot at the tail.

C. *Baby.* Make holes in an acorn with the cup on it, two at the top and two at the bottom for the arms and legs. Make a head by glueing and pressing the flat end of an acorn firmly to the top of the body. Glue cotton wool on the top of the head for hair. If you can find two small twigs with buds on the ends, push these into the holes for the arms. Push two short lengths of pipecleaners into the 'leg' holes, and bend them to make the baby sit.

D. *Jumping Man.* Use a long thread to sew the body and head together (D1), and another long thread to sew together some seeds for an arm. Push the thread through the top part of the body and sew on some more seeds for the other arm (D2). Always begin and end with a large knot. Repeat this for the legs (D3). Glue seeds on for ears.

E. *Puppy.* Glue two acorns together by their flatter ends to make the head and body. Sharpen matchsticks and push in for legs, and add a pipecleaner for a short tail. Glue on sycamore 'keys' for ears. Mark in eyes with a felt pen.

F. *Bubble Pipe.* Make a hole in the bottom of an acorn cup large enough to push in a drinking straw. Use soapy water to blow the bubbles.

ACORN NOVELTIES

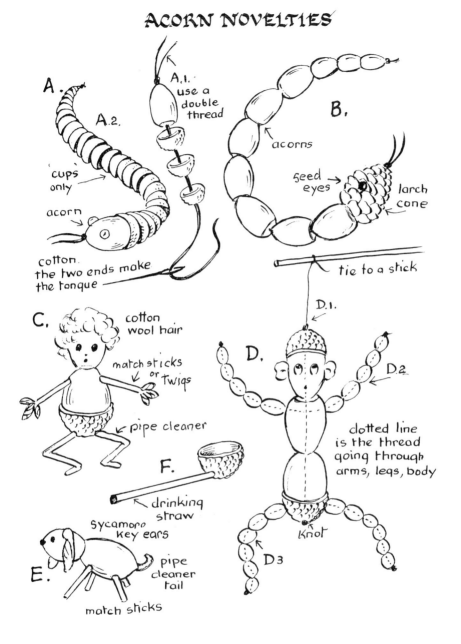

A.

A.1. use a double thread

A.2.

'cups' only

acorn

cotton. the two ends make the tongue

B.

acorns

seed eyes

larch cone

tie to a stick

D.1.

C.

cotton wool hair

match sticks or Twigs

pipe cleaner

D.

D.2

dotted line is the thread going through arms, legs, body

F.

drinking straw

Sycamore key ears

E.

pipe cleaner tail

match sticks

Knot

D.3

FUNNY CREATURES USING
HORSE-CHESTNUT SHELLS

Materials:
  a. Green or brown horse chestnut shells (conkers)
  b. Beechnuts
  c. Acorns and cups
  d. Small leaves
  e. Sycamore 'keys'
  f. Liquid glue
  g. Cardboard
  h. Pipecleaners
  i. Feathers
  j. Matchsticks
  k. Twigs
  l. Knitting needle to make holes
  m. Pins with coloured heads
  n. Plasticine

A,B, If these seed cases have fallen from the horse chestnut tree
C,D. without breaking open, keep them like that with the conker
inside. If they have fallen apart, firmly glue the sections
together again.
You can see how to make these animals from the drawings.
Sharpen one end of the sticks and matchsticks so you can
push them into the shells. Make the acorn cup feet of the
bird in the same way. Glue in position beaks, ears and small
seeds for eyes.

E. For this creature, first make a long roll of plasticine, then
flatten it and glue it onto a strip of cardboard the same
length (E1). Glue a conker head onto one end, followed by
sections of the chestnut shells. Each shell breaks into three
sections, but use only one of these each time. Glue them all
firmly onto the plasticine. Cut pipecleaners into short
lengths for legs (E2), and push these into the plasticine.
The eyes on long stalks (antennae) are pins, preferably with
coloured ball ends. The nose (E3) is a rosehip with the end
cut off to flatten it. Push a long pin through it and then into
the conker. Put a little glue on the conker to stick the hip
firmly to it.

FUNNY CREATURES USING HORSE-CHESTNUT SHELLS

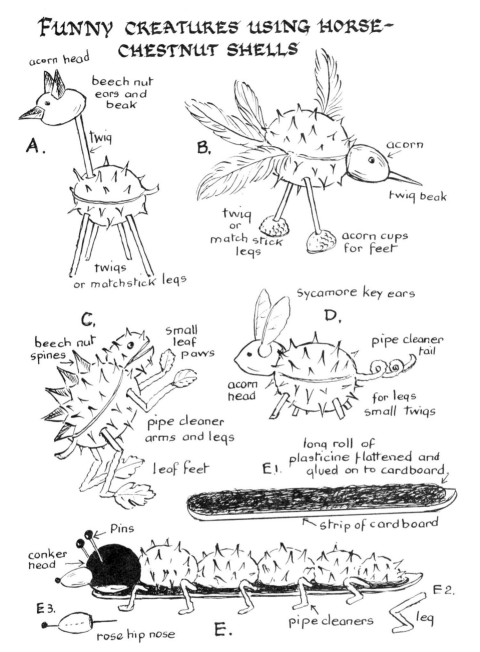

acorn head

beech nut ears and beak

twig

A.

twigs or matchstick legs

B.

acorn

twig beak

twig or match stick legs

acorn cups for feet

C.

beech nut spines

small leaf paws

pipe cleaner arms and legs

leaf feet

Sycamore key ears

D.

pipe cleaner tail

acorn head

for legs small twigs

E1. long roll of plasticine flattened and glued on to cardboard

strip of cardboard

Pins

conker head

E3.

rose hip nose

E.

pipe cleaners

E2.

leg

WALNUT SHELL TOYS

Materials:	a. Walnut shells in halves (can be bought)	
	b. Sycamore winged seeds	c. Leaf or paper
	d. Matchstick or twig	e. Green paint
	f. Beads (1 large, 3 small)	g. Thin cardboard
	h. Strong cotton or thin string	i. Small drill for hole making
	j. Pipecleaners or wire	k. Plasticine
	l. Needle	m. Scissors
	n. Liquid glue or gum	o. Felt pen

A. *Tortoise.* Ask a grown up to make a hole in both sides in one half of a walnut shell near the bottom (A1). Place the shell on the thin cardboard and draw round it (this makes the bottom of the tortoise). On this shape draw the legs, head and tail (A2) and cut out the whole shape. Draw on eyes and mouth with the felt pen. Carefully cut away the cardboard in the centre to make a hole a little larger than the bead. Thread the needle with the cotton or thin string, knotting it round one hole in the shell. Thread on the bead and push the needle through the other hole, and knot the thread round that side of the shell (A3). Place the cardboard shape over the shell and bead, and glue securely in position (A4). *To play* – place the tortoise on a slanting board and see it run down.

B. *Mouse.* This is made in the same way as the tortoise, but with only small legs on the cardboard (B1). Before glueing the base on, make a curly tail with a short length of pipecleaner and glue inside the shell. The base is glued over it (B2).

C. *Boat.* Use a leaf or cut paper for the sail. Thread it on to the matchstick mast and fix the mast to the bottom of the walnut shell with plasticine (see drawing).

D. *Basket.* Simply glue the string inside the shell on each side.

E. *Spider.* Draw round the walnut shell on cardboard as A1, but only add the head (NO legs) and cut it out. Onto this cardboard shape glue the eight legs made of pipecleaners or wire (E1). Before glueing on the cardboard shape, thread the needle with strong cotton and push it though the shell (E2) not in the centre, but nearer the head. Tie a large knot in one end of the cotton and tie the other (long) end to a stick so you can dangle the spider. Lastly, glue on the cardboard base.

WALNUT SHELL TOYS

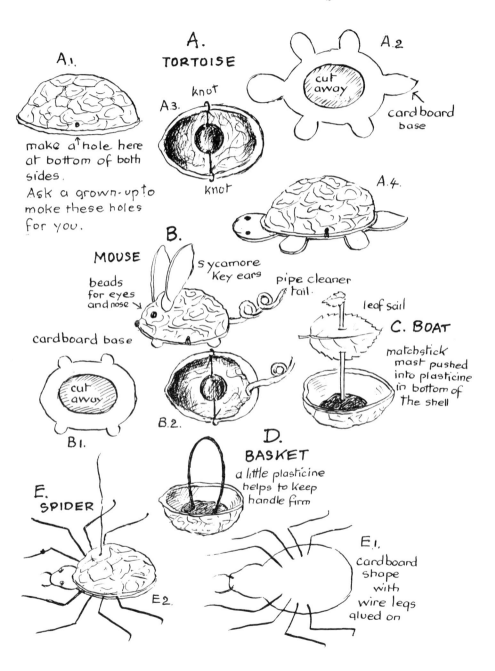

A.1.

make a hole here at bottom of both sides.
Ask a grown-up to make these holes for you.

A.
TORTOISE

A.3.
knot
knot

A.2
cut away

cardboard base

A.4.

B.
MOUSE

Sycamore Key ears

pipe cleaner tail.

beads for eyes and nose →

cardboard base

B.1.
cut away

B.2.

C. BOAT
leaf sail

matchstick mast pushed into plasticine in bottom of the shell

D.
BASKET
a little plasticine helps to keep handle firm

E.
SPIDER

E.1.
cardboard shape with wire legs glued on

E.2.

'CONKER' FURNITURE

Materials: a. Horse chestnuts (conkers)
               selecting some with flattish tops
          b. Small pins
          c. Coloured wool
          d. Needle
          e. Scissors

A.   *Chair.* Push four pins in (A1). Tie an end of the wool to the end pin, then wind it in and out of the pins as if you are weaving (A2), until you reach the tops of the pins. Then thread the needle with the end of the wool, push it down between the woven wool and cut off the end (A3). Push three pins into the base of the conker for legs (three stand firmer than four!) You can make a chair with three pins only for the back (A4).

B.   *Armchair.* Push three pins in for the back and two smaller ones in front for the arms (B1). Now wind the wool round all the pins as in A2 and fasten off. Use four pins for legs and wind wool round these too.

C.   *Stool.* This is a small conker with three or four legs wound with wool.

D.   *Table.* The table is a larger conker with eight pins pushed in flat near the top (D1). Tie the wool to one pin and then wind it round each pin as shown (*not* as A2). This will make a flatter top as in D2. Use four pins for legs.

'CONKER' FURNITURE

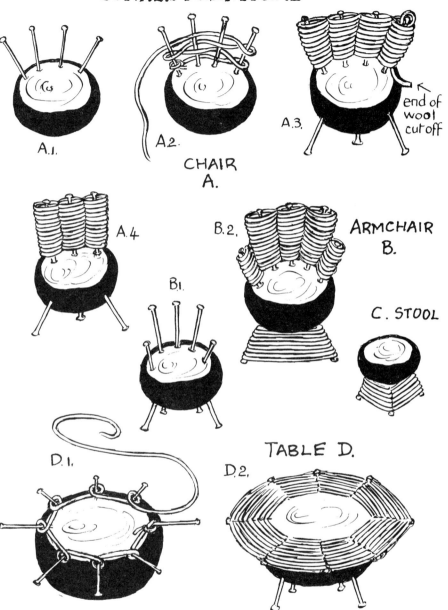

A.1.

A.2.

A.3.

end of wool cut off

CHAIR
A.

A.4

B.2.

ARMCHAIR
B.

B1.

C. STOOL

D.1.

D.2.

TABLE D.

SEED NECKLACES

Materials: a. Alder – brown catkins (cones)
            b. Red holly berries   c. Red rose hips
            d. Acorns with cups   e. Ash 'keys'
            f. Sycamore 'keys'   g. Melon seeds
            h. Beech nuts   i. Coloured drinking straws
            j. Scissors   k. Hollow green rushes
            l. Thimble   m. Needle with large eye
            n. Strong thread or cotton

Note: Do NOT use berries with hard stones in the centre, or soft squashy ones.

For each necklace thread the needle with a long strand of strong cotton or thread and push it through the seeds as shown.

A.   This necklace is made with melon seeds and cut pieces of coloured drinking straws or hollow reeds for the long beads.

B.   This has red holly berries and ash 'keys'.

C.   Red hips, beech nuts and sycamore 'keys' make up this necklace.

D.   This is made of holly berries, rose hips, acorns with cups, green hollow rushes or drinking straws. Before making it up, with needle and thread join a rose hip, rush or straw and acorn together as shown (D1) with firm knots at each end. Make several groups like this. Cut the reeds or straws into different lengths first.

Now, having made these, have fun by inventing other interesting necklaces.

SEED NECKLACES

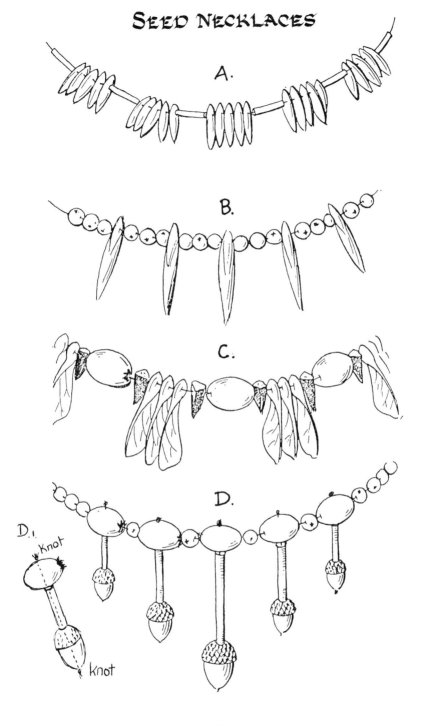

A.

B.

C.

D.

D.1.

Knot

knot

33

MORE SEED NECKLACES,
EAR-RINGS AND BRACELETS

Materials: a. Alder 'cones' (black ones)
- b. Holly berries
- c. Plane 'balls'
- d. Rose hips
- e. Elm 'winged' seeds
- f. Acorn with cup
- g. Beech nuts
- h. Melon seeds
- i. Ash 'keys'
- j. Liquid glue or gum
- k. Thin card
- l. Scissors
- m. Needle with large eye
- n. Strong thread or thin string
- o. Drinking straws or reeds
- p. 10 pence coin

A.   **Ear-ring.** Thread about six to eight holly berries on a short length of cotton thread or string, bend them round to form a ring and knot the ends of the thread firmly, leaving the ends to tie round your ear later on. Knot another thread and run it through the acorn and through a cut piece of drinking straw or reed. Tie in the centre of the holly ring and cut the end of that thread.

B.   This ear-ring is made in the same way with the alder 'cones'.

C.   Quite often plane 'balls' are already two on a stem. Leave them like that. For this necklace pass the thread or string through the holly berries, then through the top 'ball' and again on through the rest of the berries. Use as many berries as you wish.

D.   For this a bunch of ash 'keys' (left as they have grown) are sewn to a plane 'ball' which has straws and beech nuts for beads.

E.   Draw round a 10p coin to make a circle on the thin card and cut out. Glue the four elm 'winged' seeds in position (E1). Glue four hips on the card between the seeds and also a small red berry in the centre. Pass the thread with berries through the top hip, etc.

F,G, H.   These bracelets are simply seeds sewn on a length of thread or string which is then tied round in a circle to fit your arm.

SEED NECKLACES, EAR-RINGS & BRACELETS

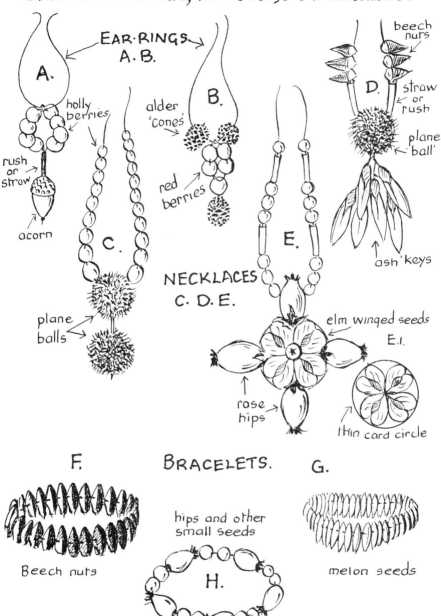

EAR-RINGS
A. B.

A.

holly berries

rush or straw

acorn

alder 'cones'

B.

red berries

beech nuts

D.

straw or rush

plane 'ball'

C.

plane balls

NECKLACES
C. D. E.

E.

ash 'keys'

elm winged seeds

E.I.

rose hips

thin card circle

F.

BRACELETS.

G.

Beech nuts

hips and other small seeds

H.

melon seeds

NECKLACES AND PENDANTS

Materials: a. Various seeds and small leaves
(used here are beech nuts, small cones,
holly berries and small leaves)
b. Plastic cut from used food container trays
(white or coloured)
c. Knitting needle   d. String (white or coloured)
e. Ruler   f. Pencil
g. Scissors   h. Liquid glue or gum
i. Small round lids etc to use as templates
to draw round

A.   For a base for any of these necklaces and pendants, cut a circle or any shape you fancy from a plastic tray. Use the knitting needle to make the hole.

B.   This pendant is simply four beech nuts with an alder cone in the centre, all glued firmly in position on a shape.

C.   This is similar to B but with a small larch cone and a leaf, or three or four small leaves.

D.   This one is a different shape with two sycamore 'keys', alder cones and a plane 'ball' glued firmly on.

E.   One large circle and five smaller ones are cut for this necklace with holes made on each as shown. These circles are tied together with small loops of string. The two last circles need longer strands to tie round the neck. The seeds and leaves are glued on last of all.

F1, F2, F3.
These are other shapes cut from plastic to use for pendants.

NECKLACES AND PENDANTS

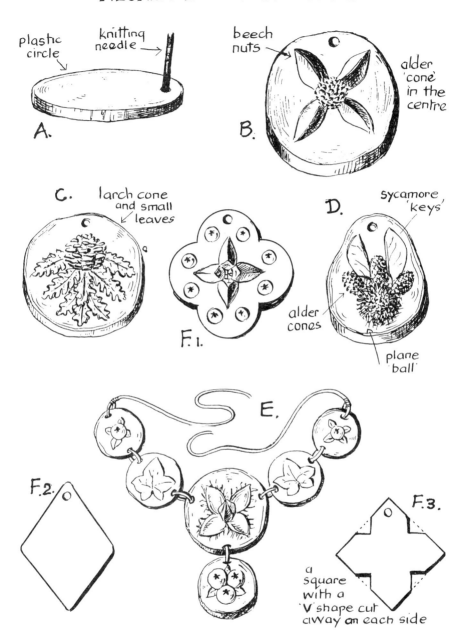

plastic circle

knitting needle →

A.

beech nuts

alder 'cone' in the centre

B.

C. larch cone and small leaves

D. sycamore 'keys'

alder cones

plane 'ball'

F.1.

E.

F.2.

F.3.

a square with a 'V' shape cut away on each side

PRESSED FLOWER PICTURES

Materials: a. Pressed flowers, leaves, ferns and grasses
             b. Cardboard or stiff paper, 253mm (10") by
                203mm (8"), this can be plain or coloured
             c. Piece of wallpaper or plain paper, 76mm (3") by
                101mm (4")
             d. Sellotape
             e. Scissors
             f. Pencil
             g. Length of ribbon, 76mm (3")
             h. Glue
             i. Ruler

Your plants must be gathered a week or two before you make these pictures. Pick small garden or wild flowers and pretty shaped leaves and ferns. Place them, arranged nicely, between sheets of newspapers and then put them under a weight for a week. Take them out carefully and replace between fresh newspapers and again under a weight for another day or two. Never let any plant or leaf touch another when pressing or they will dry stuck together.

1.   When quite dry select your plants and arrange them on the cardboard with all the stems coming to the centre. Cut small strips of sellotape to stick over the stems to keep them in place, and another strip near the heads.

2.   Fold the wallpaper in half, draw half a vase shape on it as in **3**.

3.   Cut out both sides of folded paper together and open out. Does yours look something like 4a?

4.   Paste this case over the stems of the plants, with the bottom of the vase touching the bottom of the card. Fasten the ribbon to the back with sellotape. To make a frame, rule off about 6mm (.25") from the edge and colour in.

PRESSED FLOWER PICTURES

MATERIALS.

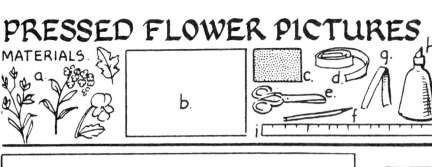

a. b. c. d. e. f. g. h. i.

1.

← sellotape

2 fold

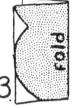

3. fold

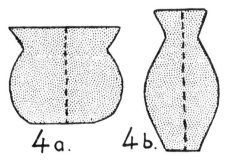

4a.   4b.

·This idea will also make
lovely calendars
Glue a calendar tab to the
picture or to ribbon under-
neath.   Cover picture
with cellophane.

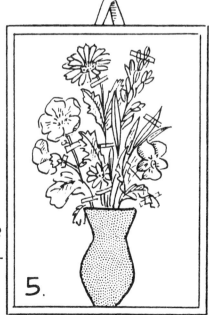

5.

WALL HANGINGS

Materials: a. All kinds of seeds will do, but here are used:

Sycamore 'keys'	Ash 'keys'
Alder 'cones' (black)	Beech nuts
Acorn cups	Lime-winged seeds
Red hips	Small cones

                Also leaves, twigs, plant seeds, seeds from fir cones

        b. Thick cardboard about 20cm x 30cm (8" x 12")

        c. Large sheet of brown, white or coloured paper

        d. Liquid gum

Note: After gathering leaves to make these patterns, before use they MUST be placed carefully between sheets of blotting or newspapers and under a weight (books are good for this) for a day or two to dry out flat. This really is a **MUST.**

A.   This hanging is on thick cardboard, coloured or plain. The seeds and twigs were arranged first to make an interesting design, then very carefully glued firmly into position. The flying insect was made using a beechnut, sycamore 'keys' and a red berry with drawn on antennae. The flower heads were small cones and various small plant seeds. Ash 'keys' for the seven-leafed part, acorn cups below, and on the right three sycamore 'keys' and small plant 'burrs'. The border was made of beech nuts glued on last of all.

B1,B2, C1, C2

These hangings can be made to any size you fancy, upright or longways. These shown are longways hangings. You can see how to arrange leaves and seeds to make easy, simple patterns. The folds in the paper help you to arrange them evenly. For B1 and B2 the paper is folded in half, then half again and when opened the creases are as in B4. For C3 the paper is folded again by bending over the four edges (a) onto the two folds of (b). When opened, it will have creases as C4. Folding like this is really easier than measuring with a ruler and drawing lines across.

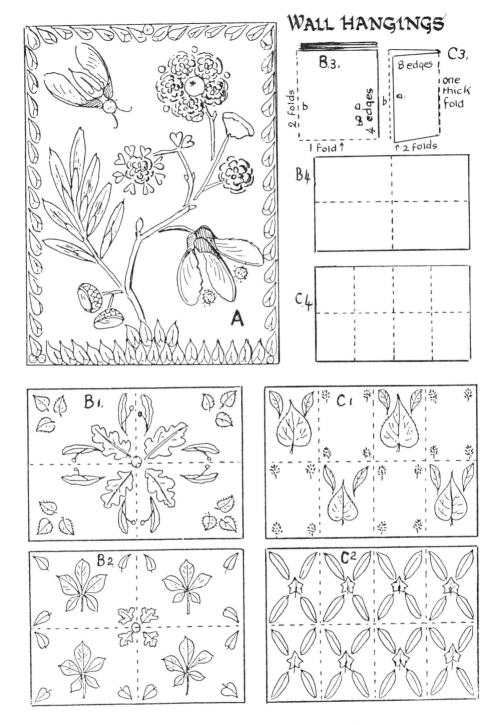

WALL HANGINGS

B.3.

2 folds
b

1 fold ↑

4 edges
a
a

8 edges

a.
b

↑ 2 folds

C3.

one thick fold

A

B4

C.4

B1.

B2.

C1.

C2.

41

MORE LEAF WALL HANGINGS

Materials: a. A large variety of leaves, of all sizes and shapes
               b. Twigs   c. Sycamore 'keys'
               d. Cardboard or   e. Liquid gum
                   strong paper   f. Ash 'keys'

Note: Read note to 'Wall Hangings' (p.40) about pressing *all* leaves before using.

These wall hangings are fun and interesting to do. Cut the cardboard or paper to the size you want, and on it arrange your leaves to make these rabbits and a bird or any other animals they suggest to you. When you like what you have arranged, stick carefully into position.

A. **Bird.** This has a large leaf for its body, long leaves to make its tail, the wing, and also the neck. Smaller leaves make the head, the tuft at the top of it, and the claws. Two thin twigs make the legs. The beak and eyes can be any small seeds you find.

B. **Rabbits.** These can have one large leaf for a body or be made up with smaller overlapping ones. One leaf makes the head. The ears are sycamore and ash 'keys' or even long leaves, and two or three small leaves make the feet and tail. Eyes can be small seeds.

MORE LEAF WALL HANGINGS

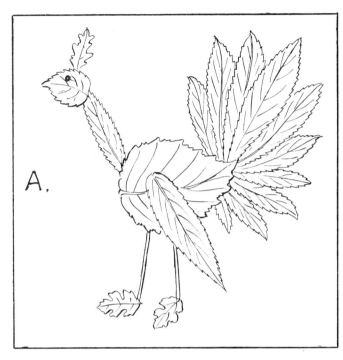

A.

Pick up
any leaves
you see,
large and
small,
also
winged
seeds for
ears and
fine twigs
for legs.

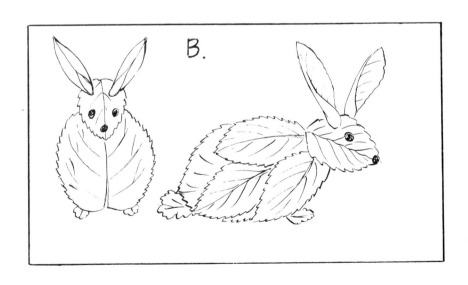

B.

LEAF PRINTS

Materials: a. Autumn leaves which have been pressed and dried off
             b. Poster paint   c. Paint brush
             d. Small shallow plastic tray or tea plate for the paint
             e. Felt or cloth, cotton wool or small sponge
             f. String   g. White plain paper
             h. Newspaper   i. Blotting paper
             j. Tweezers   k. Small stick

Autumn leaves are ideal for print-making as they are thicker and stronger to use at the end of the year rather than earlier on.

Note: The leaves must be flat. See Foreword about this.
Prints can be made in any colour and poster paint is better than ordinary water-colours.

1.   Make a small pad with a piece of felt or strong cloth tied securely round a small wad of cotton wool, or use a piece of fine sponge cut into a circle or oval without sharp edges.

2.   Put paint in the centre of the tray and gently dab the wad or sponge into it. It is best not to have too much paint on the wad until you have practised and found out how much is needed to make a good print. Too much will make a blob.

3.   Place the leaf on newspaper, back upwards with the veins showing. Hold the leaf down gently with the stick to prevent it moving when you add the paint. Carefully dab or stroke it from the centre vein out to the edges with the pad or sponge. Do this both sides from the veins outwards and don't forget the stem.

4.   Tweezers are very handy if you have any. Use them to pick the leaf up and drop it in position on the white paper, paint downwards.

5.   Place blotting paper over it and gently press down.

6.   Finally pick the leaf up with the tweezers and lay on one side to dry off.

7.   Use another for the next print. With care, leaves can be used over and over again. With practice nice prints can be made and used for gift cards, calendars, wall hangings, etc.

LEAF PRINTS

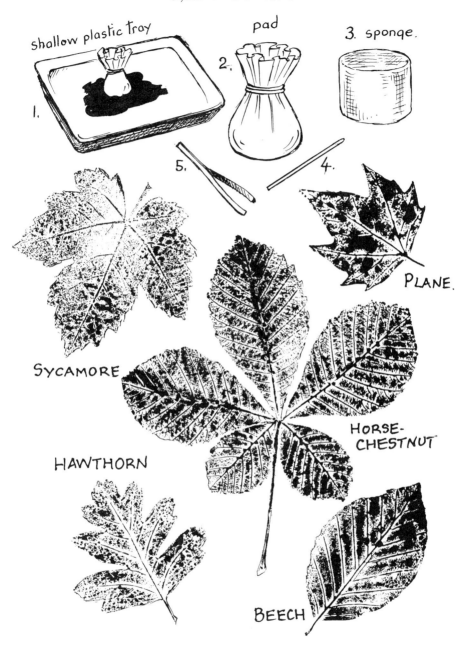

Shallow plastic tray

pad

3. sponge.

1.

2.

5.

4.

PLANE.

SYCAMORE

HORSE-
CHESTNUT

HAWTHORN

BEECH

SPATTER WITH PRESSED LEAVES

Materials: a. Leaves of attractive shapes pressed and dried
                b. Two toothbrushes   c. Blotting paper
                d. Plain pale or white cartridge papr and card
                e. Newspaper to work on
                f. Small pins   g. Poster paints
                h. Tin lids   i. Lollystick

Gather leaves and ferns for this in summer. Choose those with an attractive shape, and leave the stem on. Arrange them carefully on newspaper. They must not touch each other. Cover with more newspaper, and put a weight on them so that they dry flat. They should be prepared well in advance before using them. Use two brushes, one to mix the paint, and one to feed the other one. Spray by pointing the brush down towards the leaf, bristles uppermost. With the flat side of the lollystick gently stroke the bristles toward you. The paint will spray downwards over the leaf.

Cut and fold the paper you are using for the cards.

1a,b. Spread newspaper down to work on. Lay the card on the newspaper opened out, and cover the left-hand page with more newspaper (a). Place a fern or leaf on the right-hand side of the card with its veins uppermost. Push small pins through the tips of the points to keep them flat on the paper (b). If they are not flat on the paper, the paint will creep under the edges and make the print foggy.

2. Mix the paint in the lids to the consistency of pouring cream, and follow the instructions given above on using the two toothbrushes. Concentrate on spraying the edge of the leaf to make a good contrasting print, but do not overdo it. When satisfied, remove the pins and gently lift the leaf smartly up and away, being very careful not to smudge the wet paint.

3. With practice and care, it is possible to make both a negative and positive print with the same leaf at the same time. Have a second card ready at the side. When you are satisfied that the edge of the leaf has been sprayed enough, spray a little more in the centre if it needs it, but do not make it too wet. When you remove the leaf from the first card, drop it neatly on the second card paint side down. Put blotting paper over it and press very gently with the finger tips all over it. DO NOT thump with the fist as this could cause the leaf to move and spoil the print.

Spattered cards are very attractive and can be used for almost any occasion. The greetings can be written or pasted inside.

SPATTER WITH PRESSED LEAVES

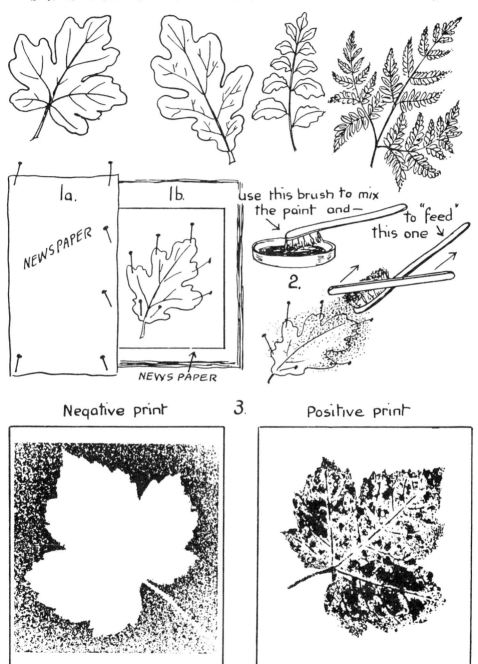

1a.

NEWSPAPER

1b.

NEWS PAPER

use this brush to mix
the paint and—

to "feed"
this one

2.

Negative print

3.

Positive print

GIFTS TO MAKE

Materials: a. A variety of seeds and leaves as seen here
             b. Cardboard plates (coloured or plain)
             c. Plastic trays from fruit or other food containers
             d. Small boxes   e. Scissors
             f. Ball of string   g. Cellophane
             h. Liquid glue   i. Gummed paper
             j. Cord, ribbon

Note: See note to 'Wall Hangings' (p. 40) about pressing *all* leaves before using for these gifts.

These items were all made by children.

A,B, C. A and B are made using plastic or cardboard trays once used for food containers. Wash these well before using to remove grease, etc. C is a larger cardboard plate. These can be bought in packets.
Arrange your seeds and leaves in any way to make a pattern that pleases you. Glue them firmly in position. When the glue has dried, turn the plates and trays over and glue on a short strand of cord or ribbon or a strip of gummed paper to make a loop for hanging them up.

D. If you want to make a calendar as a Christmas gift, buy the calendar tab and use the cord or ribbon to fasten it to hang below the plate.

E,F,G, H
These boxes make ideal gifts. E and G are based on small cardboard boxes, and F is a round cheese box. H is a tall cardboard container. To cover any wording, etc. on these boxes, stick on firmly some plain white or coloured gummed paper. When it is dry, glue your seeds and leaves on to make attractive patterns.
G is used as a string box, so has a small hole pierced in the lid for the string to pass through.

If you wish to protect these arrangements, cover them carefully with cellophane which has a sticky back.

GIFTS TO MAKE

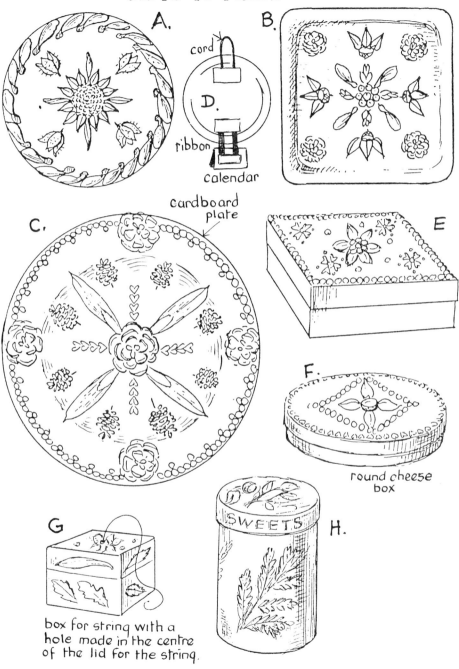

A.

B.

cord

D.

ribbon

calendar

cardboard plate

C.

E.

F.

round cheese box

G.

SWEETS

H.

box for string with a hole made in the centre of the lid for the string.

49

MORE GIFTS

Materials: a. Small cardboard carton
               b. White or coloured gummed paper
               c. White or coloured card

d. Various leaves	e. Round cheese box
f. Scissors	g. Pinking shears
h. Calendar tabs	i. Ribbon
j. Cellophane	k. Ruler
l. Pencil	m. Liquid gum

Note: See note to 'Wall Hangings' (p.40) about pressing *all* leaves before using for these gifts.

A.   ***Wastepaper 'Basket'.*** This is based on a cardboard carton. Remove the lid flaps and cut the edges smoothly. Cover each side of the box with white or coloured paper, leaving an extra overlap at the top to fold over and stick down inside the box (A1). Select your leaves, large or small, and stick carefully on each side of the box. Finally, cover with cellophane for protection.

B.   ***Calendar.*** Cut a long strip of card. Choose a nice spray of leaves and stick in position. Cut a strip of ribbon long enough to stick to the back of the card and cover the ends with a strip of gummed paper (B1). The calendar tab can be stuck to the bottom of the card or made to hang below with one or two strips of ribbon fixed to the back of the card and calendar tab as in B2 and B3.

C.   ***Calendar.*** A round cheese box makes an attractive calendar. Lay the box on the white or coloured gummed paper and draw round it. Cut out this circle and stick it on to the lid to cover it. Cut a long, narrow strip to cover the side of the box. Put gum on the inside of the rim and stick it firmly over the bottom of the box. Arrange a leaf spray or small leaves in a pattern and stick them on to the round top. Add strips of ribbon to make a hanging loop and also to attach the calendar as for B1, B2 and B3.

D.   ***Book Marker.*** Cut the edge of a strip of thin card with pinking shears. Stick on small leaves in a simple pattern.

Cover all these gifts with cellophane to protect them.

MORE GIFTS

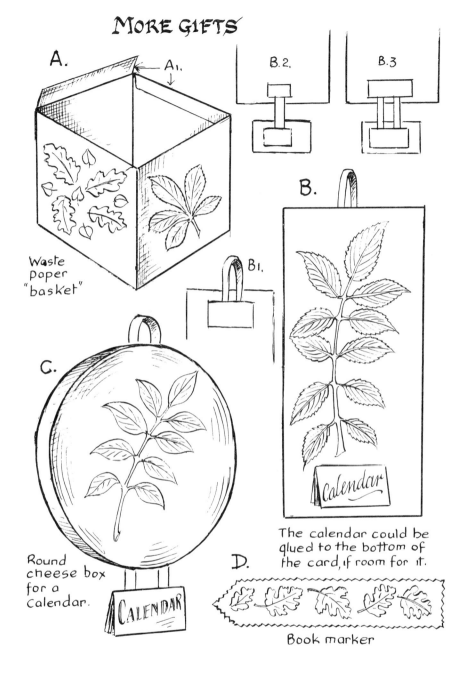

A. A₁.

B.2.   B.3

Waste paper "basket"

B.

B1.

C.

Round cheese box for a calendar.

CALENDAR

Calendar

The calendar could be glued to the bottom of the card, if room for it.

D.

Book marker

CHRISTMAS CANDLEHOLDER

Materials: a. Plasticine   b. Beech mast
              c. Lichen   d. Small candle
              e. Paints   f. Matchstick

This idea comes from Denmark.

1.   Before you can make this you must go out and gather up a few of the prickly seed cases you will find under beech trees. They are called beech mast.

2.   You also want some of the green-grey growth which you see on some tree trunks and branches – the kind that looks like whiskers or long fingers! This is lichen.

3.   Paint the inside of the beech mast, red, green or white. Poster paint is best and when rubbed on soap with the brush it will go on much more easily.

4.   Make a ball of plasticine, rolling it in your hands to make it round.

5.   Put this on a newspaper-covered table and push the candle into the centre. This will flatten the plasticine on the bottom and make the holder stand firm.

6.   Use the matchstick to push the lichen into the plasticine. Cover all the surface quite thickly.

7.   Push three or four pointed beech masts round the candle, and the holder is finished.

This can be made in exactly the same way using clay instead of plasticine; the clay, when it hardens, makes a permanent holder.

CHRISTMAS CANDLEHOLDER

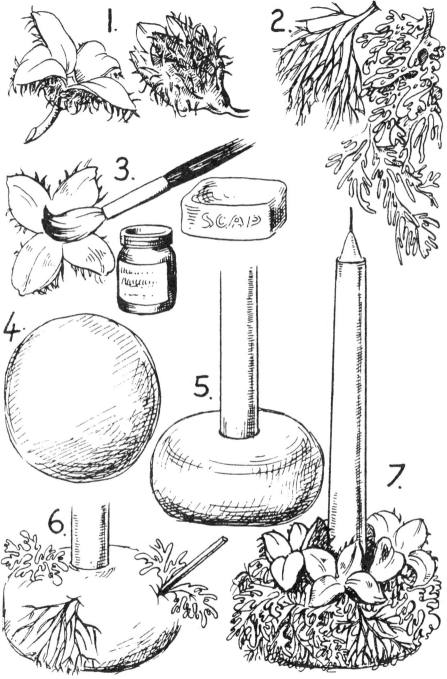

53

LEAF FANS

Materials: a. Long and shorter leaves
              b. Scissors   c. Newspaper
              d. Stiff cardboard   e. Plate or saucer
              f. Glue   g. Pencil
              h. Gummed paper   i. Cellophane
              j. Pinking shears (optional)

1. Lay the plate or saucer on the cardboard and draw round it.

2. Lay the same plate or saucer on newspaper, draw round it and cut out the circle (a). Now fold this paper circle in half and crease it (b). Cut along the fold. This will give you two half circles.

3. Lay one half circle over the cardboard circle you drew and with your pencil draw along the straight line. Cut out the cardboard circle and along the centre line to get two half circles to make two fans (A).

4. On one of the cardboard half circles glue the long leaves. They will overlap a little on the straight edge (B1).

5. Very carefully glue a second set of long leaves over the first ones to fill the gap at the top of the circle (B2).

6. About halfway down glue smaller leaves (C1 and C2) and then smaller ones still at the bottom (D1 and D2).

7. Cut a strip of gummed paper long enough to go across the bottom of the fan and wide enough to bend under and up to stick to the back of the fan (D3). This is to protect the bottom leaves.

8. With scissors make small V-shapes on the cardboard edge which may show between the long leaves, or use pinking shears to cut a zigzag round the half circle of card *before* glueing the leaves on.

9. Now make another fan with the other half circle!

10. Protect the leaves if you like with cellophane cut to fit the half circle.

Leaf Fans

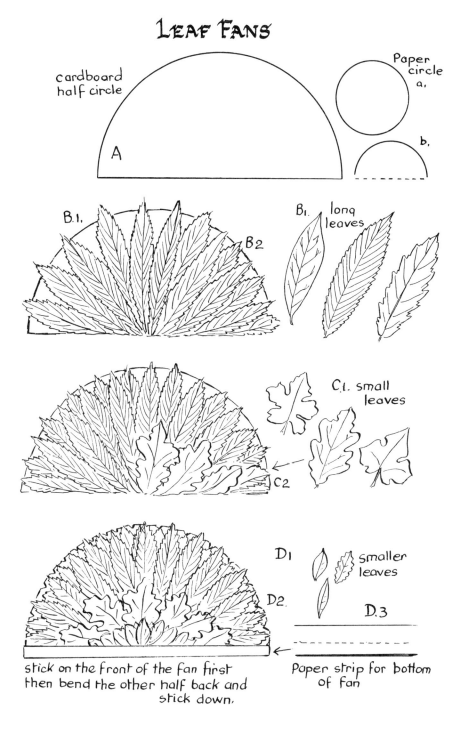

cardboard
half circle

Paper
circle
a,

b,

A

B.1.

B2

B1. long
leaves

C.1. small
leaves

C2

D1

D2.

smaller
leaves

D.3

stick on the front of the fan first
then bend the other half back and
stick down,

Paper strip for bottom
of fan

55

REED OR STRAW DOLL

Materials: a. Several reeds or straws about 15cm (6") long
             b. Wool or string
             c. Scissors

A.   Gather the reeds together. You can make them any size but 15cm (6") long is a good size to begin with.

B.   Tie wool round the reeds about 2.5cm (1") from the top, and again the same length below.

C.   Gather some of the reeds up on each side to make the arms. Cut them a little shorter. Then tie the wool round to make the hands.

D.   For the body, tie wool round the reeds about 3cm (1.25") from the head.

E.   To make a lady doll, simply pull the reeds apart to make a skirt. Also fluff out the top of the reeds on the head to make hair.

F.   For a gentleman doll divide the reeds in half and tie wool round for feet. Pull out the reeds at the top for his hair.

With many more straws these dolls can be made larger to use at Harvest Festivals.

REED OR STRAW DOLL

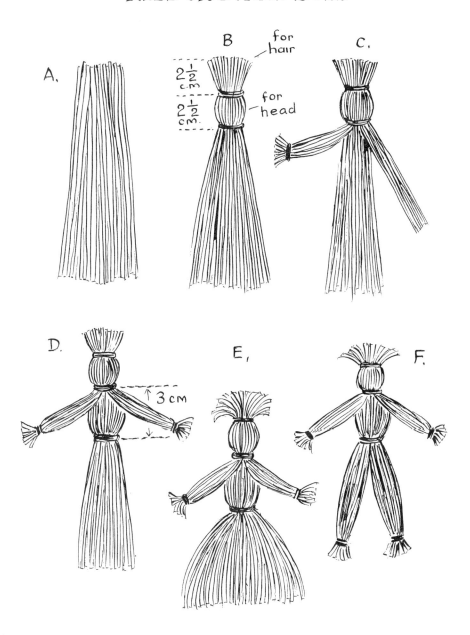

A.

B.

$2\frac{1}{2}$ c.m.

$2\frac{1}{2}$ cm.

for hair

for head

C.

D.

↑ 3 cm

E,

F.

REED OR STRAW RATTLE

Materials: a. Reeds or straws roughly about 12cm (5") long
    b. Wool
    c. Marble or small stone
    d. Small round box with a lid
    e. Glue   f. Scissors
    g. Ribbon   h. Brown paper
    i. Needle with large eye

A. Gather reeds or straws into a bundle cut about 12cm (5") long.

B. Knot and then firmly bind the wool round the reeds, from the bottom to about halfway up. This forms the handle.

C. Knot and tie the wool firmly off. Thread the needle with the loose end and push it down inside the binding. Cut it off at the bottom.

D. Use a small box, about 3cm (1.5") in diameter, with a lid. Put the marble or stone inside it and glue the lid on firmly.

Note: Do NOT put a box or round container in the rattle without a lid, but cover the top of a lidless box right over with strong brown paper and glue it securely on.

E. Open out the reeds at the top of the handle and put the box inside them. Arrange the reeds neatly and evenly all round.

F1. Gather the reeds together and bind firmly at the top with wool.

F2. To make the reeds firmer round the top of the box and to prevent them pulling apart when rattled, thread the needle and sew them all round as in F2. Then tie the wool ends together tightly.
Make sure that the wool work in F2 really is firm and not loose before giving the rattle to the baby.

G. If you like, decorate the handle with a firmly tied bow of narrow ribbon.

REED OR STRAW RATTLE

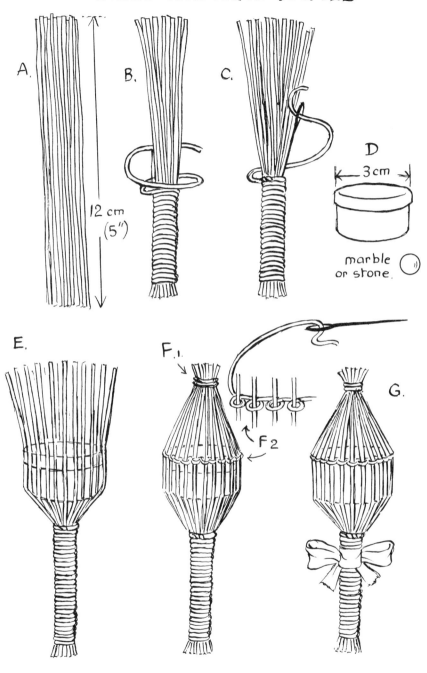

A.

12 cm
(5")

B.

C.

D
3 cm

marble
or stone.

E.

F.1

F.2

G.

BURDOCK DARTS AND FISHBONES

Materials: a. Burdock seed heads ('burrs')
               b. Feathers
               c. Knitting needle
               d. Square of felt or old blanket
               e. White chalk
               f. Ruler
               g. Horse chestnut leaves

A,B. *Burdock Dart and Dartboard.* Burdocks are usually found on waste ground and in the country. They look like thistles until you look closely and see that their heads are covered with hooks (A1 and A2). These hooks cling to everything so make good darts.

With the knitting needle make a hole in the bottom of the burr (where the stalk was). Into it push the bird's feather (A3). That is all there is to it – simple!

For fun and a game, mark off a piece of felt with chalk. It can be square as (B) and numbered, or round and marked as a dartboard. Hang it up to play.

C. *'Fishbones' from Horse Chestnut Leaves.* Hold the leaf in one hand, and with the other hand very carefully and gently put your forefinger and thumb on the leaf near the long centre vein (C1), and between the side veins. Slowly pull the leaf away between the side veins, leaving them intact and looking like a 'fishbone'. Do this along both sides of the leaf to make it look like C2.

Have a competition to see who can make the best one.

BURDOCK DARTS. 'FISHBONES'

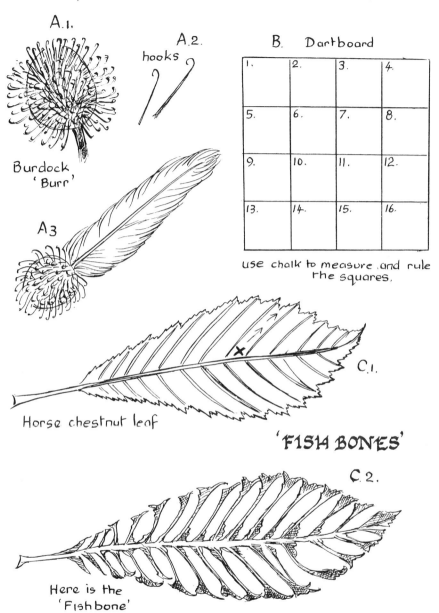

A.1.

Burdock 'Burr'

A.2.

hooks

A3

Horse chestnut leaf

B. Dartboard

1.	2.	3.	4.
5.	6.	7.	8.
9.	10.	11.	12.
13.	14.	15.	16.

use chalk to measure and rule the squares.

C.1.

'FISH BONES'

C.2.

Here is the 'Fishbone'

CONE 'WEATHER' VANES

Materials: a. Large, long fir cones   b. Two small winged seeds
                c. Acorn with its cup   d. Knitting needle
                e. Plasticine   f. Felt pen (black)
                g. Liquid glue or gum   h. Small square of card
                i. Plastic container top large enough to fit a cone

A.   *Tree.* This is very simple. The large cone A1 is placed in the plastic top, to make sure it fits. Then the plasticine is pressed firmly into the plastic top (A2). Push on the bottom of the cone. It may help to hold the cone even firmer if you put glue round the top of the plastic container.

B.   *Figure.* This cone is used upside down (B1). Make a hole in the acorn with the knitting needle (B2) and push the short stump of cone stem into it, putting glue round the stem and the cone so it sticks to the acorn.
Make two small rolls of plasticine and flatten them on to the small square of cardboard. These make feet for the cone. Put glue on the end of the cone and push it well into the plasticine. Leave to dry until it is quite firm. Then glue small winged seeds onto the head for ears and draw on features with the black felt pen.

When all the glued parts of the tree and figure are really dry, the cone scales will tell you what the weather will be. If it is a fine day, the scales will open wide; if it is to be a wet day, the scales will close.

CONE 'WEATHER' VANES

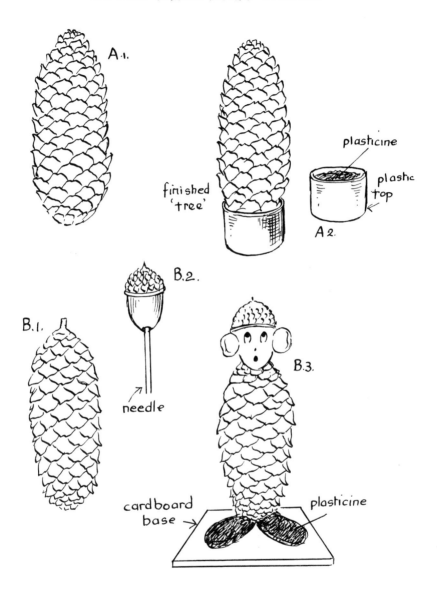

A.1.

finished 'tree'

plasticine

plastic top

A 2.

B.1.

B.2.

needle

B.3.

cardboard base

plasticine

AMERICAN INDIAN LEAF HEADDRESS

Materials: a. Long and smaller leaves
               b. Elm seeds, red berries or other seeds
                   for decoration
               c. Liquid glue or gum
               d. Corrugated cardboard

A,B,C.

Measure the head the headband is to fit and from the corrrugated cardboard cut the strip about 4cm (1.75") wide, and long enough to go round the head, with an extra 5cm (2") for overlap (A). Bend it into a circle and glue together with the smooth part outside (B).
Stick the seeds on to the headband to make a pattern (C1). C2 shows an attractive pattern using elm seeds: a red berry could be used in the centre.

D.   When the seeds are firmly fixed, push a long leaf into the slotted sections in the front, and add others not so long in the slots at either side of the first one. Push in smaller leaves to fill the gaps between the long leaves.

AMERICAN INDIAN LEAF HEAD-DRESS

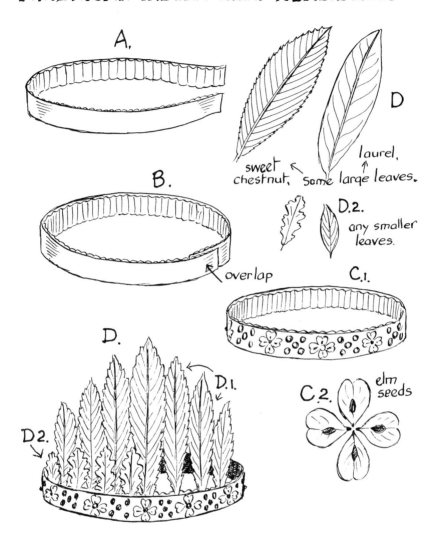

A.

B.

overlap

C.1.

D

sweet chestnut.

laurel,
some large leaves.

D.2.
any smaller leaves.

D.

D.1.

D2.

C.2. elm seeds

65

RUSH WHIP

Materials: a. Rushes (not too short)
             b. Ball of wool
             c. Needle with large eye
             d. Scissors

A. Arrange the rushes neatly with the thicker ends together.

B. Knot a length of wool firmly round the thick ends and wind it round and round tightly to make the handle. Fasten it off with a firm knot.

C1. Cut a length from the ball of wool and thread the needle with it. Push it down inside the binding; this will keep the loose end out of the way.

C2. Plait the loose ends of the reeds. You will find the plait will get smaller as you go along because the reeds are not so thick at the end. Tie the ends together firmly.

Below the drawing opposite is a rhyme children used to say about rushes.

RUSH WHIP

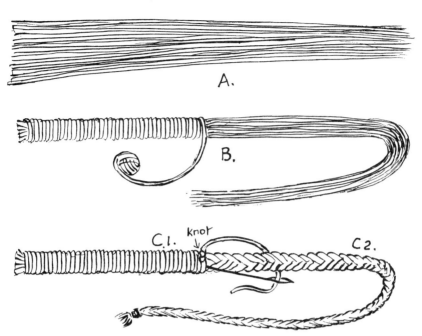

A.

B.

C.1. knot C.2.

" Green grow the rushes, O!
To make our whips
And farthing dips,
Green grow the rushes, O! "

'Farthing dips' were night-lights made
from rushes and used in very early days.
A farthing was a small coin.

'CONKERS' GAME

Materials: a. Good-sized horse chestnuts
(one for each player)
b. A length of string for each conker
c. Knitting needle or bradawl

A.   Carefully push the knitting needle or bradawl through the
conker, from top to bottom, without splitting it.
Push the string through and tie a large double knot in one
end.

To play this game, whoever manages to say first the sentence –
"Iddy, iddy O, my first go!" has the chance to strike first
(alternatively, you can toss a coin). The other player holds
the conker up by the string (B2).
The one who starts, has to swing the conker and strike as
hard as possible trying to hit the other one (B1). Each player
strikes in turn, the game being to smash the other conker if
possible.
The winner is the 'conker of one', that is, he or she has
smashed one conker. The game continues if the loser holds
up a new conker but the winner must use his 'conker of one'
to see if he can win again with it and make his winning
conker a 'conker of two' ... and so on to see how often he can
use the same conker to smash others.

The rhyme is one the players used to say when playing this
game.

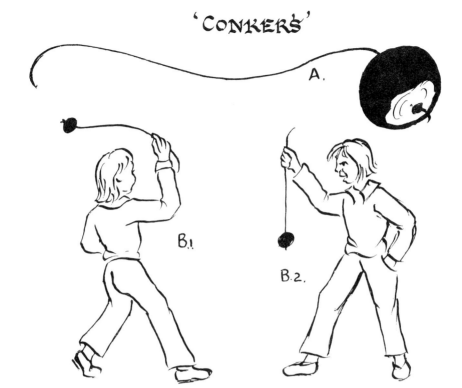

" Iddy, iddy onker my first conker,
Iddy, iddy O, my first go "

" With a stout piece of string
and with chestnuts for men,
We'll fight and we'll conquer
again and again !

PLANTAIN 'CHAMPIONS'
(TWO GAMES)

Materials: One plantain seed head on a long stem for each player for each round.

Game One

A.   Use a plantain like this with a long stem for both games.

B1.   Twist the lower end of the stem up and over near the head.

B2.   With one hand hold the lower end, and the twisted part with the other hand.

B3.   Then quickly move the upper hand forward to the top in an attempt to 'shoot' the head off to hit the other player.

This is a simple game to see who hits the other player the most often with the plantain heads and so becomes the winner.

Game Two

C.   Each player has a plantain. This game is played like 'conkers', each player taking it in turns to strike at the other player's plantain to break off its head.

    The winner uses his plantain a second time and if successful uses it again, saying the first verse of this rhyme shown opposite.
If the winner is successful a third time, he quotes both verses.

PLANTAIN 'CHAMPIONS' 2 GAMES

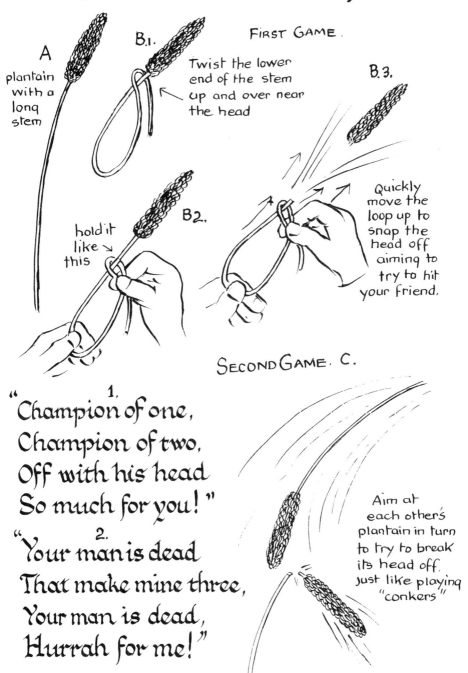

FIRST GAME.

A — plantain with a long stem

B.1. — Twist the lower end of the stem up and over near the head

B2. — hold it like this

B.3. — Quickly move the loop up to snap the head off aiming to try to hit your friend.

SECOND GAME. C.

Aim at each other's plantain in turn to try to break its head off. Just like playing "conkers"

1.
"Champion of one,
Champion of two,
Off with his head
So much for you!"

2.
"Your man is dead
That make mine three,
Your man is dead,
Hurrah for me!"

ASH LEAVES AND CLOVER
FOR GOOD LUCK RHYMES

ASH LEAVES.

When out for a walk, see if there are fallen ash leaves lying on the ground. Look carefully and, as the rhyme says, if you find one with an *even* number of small side leaves (B), you are in luck. This does not often happen as each leaf is made up of an odd number of small side leaflets as in A – perhaps of five, seven or eleven. *Never* remove a small leaf to make an even number or you really will have 'BAD LUCK'. One which *grows* with an even number is *your* luck.

FOUR-LEAFED CLOVER

Although clovers bloom all summer, they finish doing so about October, but the leaves are still there. Look carefully and see if you can find one with four leaves all together as in C. (Usually there are only three leaves.)

A four-leafed clover is luck indeed.

ASH LEAF, CLOVER, FOR GOOD LUCK

ASH LEAF

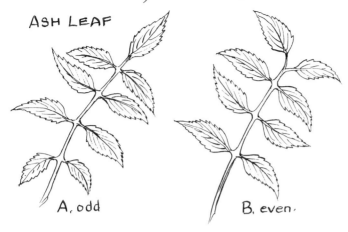

A, odd   B, even.

" Even Ash, 1 thee pick up
Hoping thou will bring me luck. "

FOUR LEAFED CLOVER

C.

"Ah! 1 see a four
leafed clover,
Now my bad luck
is over. "

WILLOW – and a RIDDLE
ABOUT ANOTHER TREE

A.   *The Willow* grows along river banks and streams, or most
places where it is damp. As the rhyme states, it is used to
make cricket bats, hurdles and whistles, and many other
things as well; baskets, chairs, weaving, and so on.

B.   *The Riddle.* This is a very old rhyme and it was said when
this particular tree was covered in red berries in the
autumn. Children soon learnt which tree it was and looked
out for it when walking through fields, lanes and gardens.
If you are not sure what the tree is from the picture, the
answer is printed upside down below the riddle, with the
name of the seed also.

WILLOW, AND A RIDDLE

"Cricket bats, hurdles
and whistles for me,
All of them come from
the old willow tree."

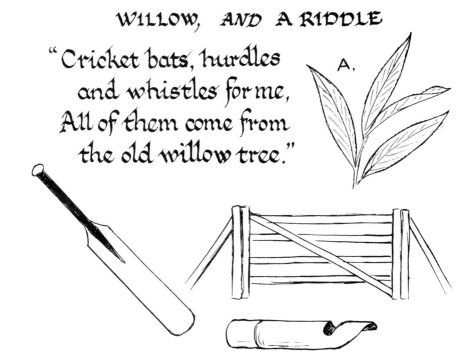

A.

A RIDDLE.   *What tree is this?*   B.

"In yonder field there stands old Pat,
In a little red jacket and a little black hat,
With a stone in his tummy
And a stick at his back,
In yonder field there
stands old Pat."

The Hawthorn, 'Pat' is a Haw.

ANOTHER RIDDLE

What Is The Answer?

This is a similar kind of riddle, but it is the translation of a very old German rhyme.

As with the riddle on the previous page, it was quoted to the children in the autumn when they looked for the 'little man'.

Can you recognise the tree and its seed? It has been mentioned at the beginning of the book and its seeds are used in the making of different things.

Do you know what the tree is?
You will find the answer written upside down below the drawings.

A little man stands in the woods
    so still and quiet,
He is wearing a little coat bright red.
Say, who might be this little man
    in his bright red coat
All alone in the woods?

A little man stands in the woods
    on one leg,
He is wearing a little black cap on his head,
Say, who might be this little man with
 his little black cap on his head
All alone in the woods?

A German Rhyme.

The Dog Rose. *The little man is a 'Hip'.*

CHERRY EAR-RINGS AND
FIGHTING COCKS TOY

A. **Cherries.** Here is a very old rhyme that small children
    loved to say. They also used to wear cherries as ear-rings.
    As you can see you must have two cherries which meet
    together by their stems at the top. You then just slip these
    over your ears as shown. Push any long hair out of the way.

B. **Fighting Cocks**. Here is a simple toy to make using a
    hairpin or pipecleaner bent in half. Any large seed or nut
    will do for the cock's heads: here, rose hips, or acorns
    without the cup have been used, and small feathers or
    leaves pushed and gummed into small holes made by a
    needle. Beech nuts make good beaks and small beads or
    seeds make eyes. The wire or pipecleaner is pushed in the
    heads.

    To make them 'fight' just hold the wire or pipecleaner
    between thumb and forefinger and push together.

CHERRY EAR-RINGS

"Ladies have ear-rings – ruby red:
I have cherries, and so I said
Cherries would do for me instead
For ripe cherries are ruby red."

A.

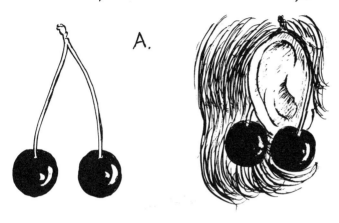

B. FIGHTING COCKS *for fun*

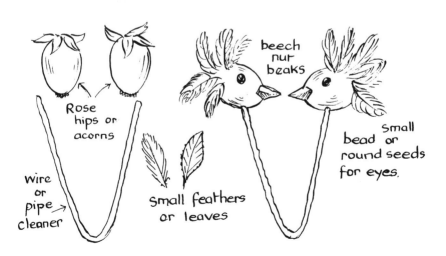

Rose
hips or
acorns

beech
nut
beaks

small
bead or
round seeds
for eyes.

Wire
or
pipe
cleaner

small feathers
or leaves

DANDELION CLOCKS AND CHAIN

A. **Dandelion Clock**. There cannot be many children, even today, who have not blown the seeds off a dandelion's head to see what the time might be. This is a very old game played years ago and there are still lots of seed heads to blow, especially in autumn, and found almost anywhere.

B. **Dandelion Chains**. When the seeds have been blown off a dandelion, they leave the dead head as in (a). These are what are used to make the chains, as their stems are hollow (b). They are very simple to make. Snap or cut the head off. The stems are narrower at the top, so bend them round and push that narrow end well into the wider hole at the other end (c). Make one 'link' to start with, then make the chain by fastening each link together as in (d). Make it as short or as long as you wish.

DANDELION CLOCKS

"What's the time ? what's the time ?
Blow, and we shall see — one o'clock,—
two o'clock — three o'clock — four o'clock
— five o'clock, time for tea —
six o'clock — seven o'clock,
Time for bed for me ! "

A.

DANDELION CHAIN   B.

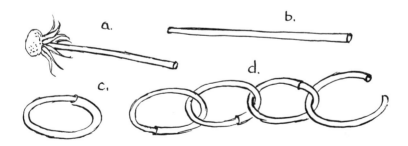

a.

b.

c.

d.

RYE GRASS

This game is still played by children who pull a seed head off the rye-grass when saying the rhymes, and repeating it until all the seeds are pulled off. Then, with another grass they say another rhyme and so on.

1.   There are slightly different wordings said in different parts of the country.

2.   With another rye grass, No.2 rhyme is said and repeated until all the seed heads are off, and so on with a new rye grass for each rhyme.

This rhyming game can be played with cherry or other fruit stones left on the plate after eating a pudding.

RYE GRASS (What will my lover be?)

1. "Tinker, tailor **or** "Soldier, sailor,
   soldier, sailor,   tinker, tailor,
   rich man,   gentle-man,
   poor man,   apothecary,
   beggar-man,   plough-boy,
   THIEF!"   THIEF!"

2.
"When will my true
love marry me?
This year – next year
– some time? –
NEVER!"

3.
"Of what will my
wedding dress
be made? Silk,
satin – muslin –
RAGS!"

4.
"What will our
wedding transport
be? Coach,
carriage,
wheel barrow,
DUST CART!"

5.
"Where will the
wedding service be?
Cathedral,
church, chapel
synagogue,
REGISTRY OFFICE!"

BANANA BOAT TOY

Materials: a. A well shaped banana with a firm skin
                b. Plasticine
                c. Matchsticks
                d. A longer stick
                e. Paper to make the sail or leaf
                f. Scissors

This is not an autumn 'seed' like the others in this book, but so many bananas are in the shops at this time – so why not make use of one.

A.   Choose a well shaped banana.

B.   Very carefully peel away the top part of the banana or cut it away with scissors.

C.   Press three balls of plasticine into the bottom and press a matchstick on top of the two end balls of plasticine as in C to keep the sides of the boat in shape. The longer stick is the mast, so push that into the centre ball of plasticine.

D.   Make a small sail from a square of paper, or use a leaf and push onto the mast. Glue a small flag to the top.

A BANANA BOAT

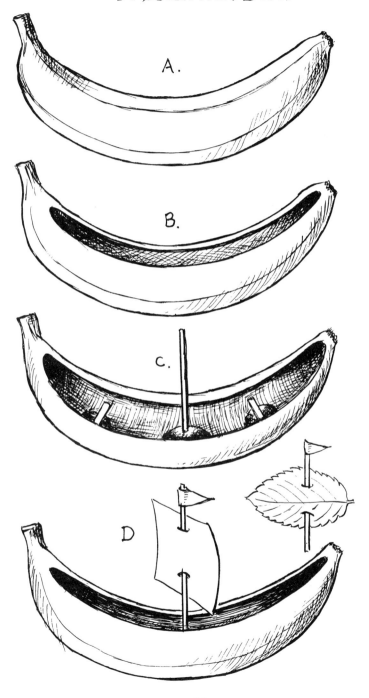

A.

B.

C.

D.

ANOTHER RIDDLE

This was a rhyme that children learnt to say for fun.

The answer is not an autumn seed but it was in use at this time of year, when the nights were long and dark. Many were used years ago before gas and electricity etc came into use for lighting. It seemed a good rhyme to end all these autumn activities.

ANOTHER RIDDLE

"Little Nancy Etticoat
In her white petticoat,
And with a red nose —
The longer she lives,
The shorter she grows."

What is she?

A candle – of course!

For a complete list of our handcraft books, please write to:

DEPT EP
JADE PUBLISHERS
15 STOATLEY RISE
HASLEMERE
SURREY GU27 1AF